Garden Tools

by John Murphy
illustrated by Olivia Cole

Practice Decodable 71

McGraw Hill Education

Bothell, WA • Chicago, IL • Columbus, OH • New York, NY

MHEonline.com

Send all inquiries to:
McGraw-Hill Education
8787 Orion Place
Columbus, OH 43240

ISBN: 978-0-02-145052-7
MHID: 0-02-145052-8

Printed in the United States of America.

7 8 9 CTM 23

Mom sat on a stool. Emily held Mom's garden tools.

"Tender shoots need room to grow. When roots get strong, the plants will bloom," Mom explained.

Mom said, "These smooth starts look droopy. Spray them to perk them up."

Amy zoomed past with an airplane. She made it swoop and loop the loop.

Mom said, "It is noon. We will go in soon." Amy's mood turned gloomy.

"What happened, Emily?" asked Mom.

"Amy looked droopy, so I tried to perk her up," said Emily.